Courage

BY CYNTHIA AMOROSO

Published by The Child's World®
1980 Lookout Drive • Mankato, MN 56003-1705
800-599-READ • www.childsworld.com

Acknowledgments
The Child's World®: Mary Berendes, Publishing Director
The Design Lab: Design
Pamela J. Mitsakos: Photo Research
Christine Florie: Editing

Photographs ©: Brand X Pictures: 11; David M. Budd Photography: 7, 9, 15, 17; iStockphoto.com/DIGIcal: cover, 1; iStockphoto.com/Imageegaml: 5; iStockphoto.com/RonTech2000:13; iStockphoto.com/Funwithfood:19; iStockphoto.com/ParkerDeen: 21

ISBN 9781623235161
LCCN 2013931773

Printed in the United States of America
Mankato, MN
July, 2013
PA02172

ABOUT THE AUTHOR

Cynthia Amoroso is Director of Curriculum and Instruction for a school district in Minnesota. She enjoys reading, writing, gardening, traveling, and spending time with friends and family.

Table of Contents

What Is Courage?   4

Courage at School   6

Making New Friends   8

Learning New Sports   10

Putting on a Show   12

Saying "I'm Sorry"   14

Being Responsible   16

Doing Something Scary   18

Courage Makes You Stronger   20

Glossary   22

Learn More   23

Index   24

What Is Courage?

There are many scary things in life. Maybe you are scared to climb the big slide at the park. Maybe you are afraid of the dark. Courage is having the strength to beat your fears. Courage is being brave!

Facing your fears shows a lot of courage!

Courage at School

It takes courage to stand up to your classmates.

Imagine that you are taking a test. Your friend wants

to **copy** your answers. You are scared to say no.

You are afraid your friend will not like you anymore.

You show courage by saying no—and by telling your

friend it is wrong to copy.

Telling a friend that copying is wrong takes courage.

Making New Friends

It takes courage to make new friends. Maybe you see a new student eating alone at lunchtime. You might be scared to talk to him. You show courage by sitting with him and talking to him. Your courage can help you make more friends!

It can take courage to talk to someone new.

Learning New Sports

It takes courage to learn new things. You might be afraid to try something new. Maybe there is a sport you are scared to try. You are afraid you might get hurt or look silly. You show courage by trying the sport. Maybe you will like it and have fun!

11

Putting on a Show

It takes courage to do things in front of people.

Maybe your piano teacher is having a **recital**.

You might be scared to play in front of people.

You think people will laugh if you play poorly.

You show courage by going on stage and

doing your best.

Playing in front of other people takes courage.

Saying "I'm Sorry"

It takes courage to say "I'm sorry" after a fight. Maybe you and a friend had a big fight. You said mean things to your friend. Your friend said things that hurt your feelings, too. You are scared to be the first one to apologize. You show courage by calling your friend and making up.

It takes courage to say that you were wrong.

Being Responsible

It takes courage to be **responsible**. Imagine that you and your sister are wrestling. You knock over and break your mother's special vase. You might be scared to tell your mother what happened. You are afraid she will be angry. You are afraid you will get into trouble. You show courage by telling your mother—even if it means you might be punished.

It takes courage to be honest about your mistakes.

Doing Something Scary

It takes courage to do something scary. Maybe you are afraid to swim. You do not like to put your head underwater. You show courage by taking swimming lessons. Maybe you will like swimming after all!

Many things that seem scary turn out to be fun!

Courage Makes You Stronger

Showing courage can be hard. It means doing something that is a little scary. But showing courage helps you test yourself. It helps you learn new things. Courage helps you grow and makes you feel good!

Showing courage helps you grow up!

Glossary

apologize—When you apologize, you say "I'm sorry."

copy—When you copy something, you do it exactly as it is done somewhere else.

punished—Being punished is getting in trouble for doing something bad.

recital—In a recital, you perform in front of other people.

responsible—Being responsible means being able to choose between right and wrong.

Learn More

Books

Leffler, Marann. *Bravery Soup*. Morton Grove, IL: A. Whitman, 2002.

Quay, Emma. *Puddle Jumping: A Book about Bravery*. New York: Dial Books for Young Readers, 2011.

Waber, Bernard. *Courage*. Boston, MA: Houghton Mifflin, 2002.

Web Sites

Visit our Web site for links about courage: childsworld.com/links

Note to Parents, Teachers, and Librarians: We routinely verify our Web links to make sure they are safe and active sites. So encourage your readers to check them out!

Index

Apologizing, 14

Copying, 6

Family, 16
fear, 4, 6, 10, 12, 14, 16, 18, 20
friends, 6, 8, 14

Punished, 16

Recital, 12
responsible, 16

School, 6
sports, 10
strength, 4
swimming, 18